If you think nothing could be more technicolor, juicy, and full of signifiers come to life than Los Angeles, you have not met (or read) Jennifer Hasegawa's NAOMIE ANOMIE: *A Biography of Infinite Desire.* These voluptuous neon lyrics bring you from the infinite loop of its first circular poem into "megatons of ocean" to the gut kick of "you don't know what things are until you break them." The taking of the innate, the floral, the paradisiacal—the arrival of Cook in Hawai'i—this violence is at the heart of Hasegawa's poems. In such a world, there's nowhere to look: sun-dried remnants of narrative, disembodied voices. The father in the poems, he combs "the white curls/steaming from/the forest floor." You stay on the ride and the poet says, "Psychopomp, ferry her."

—Cynthia Arrieu-King, author of *Continuity, Futureless Languages, and Manifest*, winner of the Gatewood Prize

In *NAOMIE ANOMIE*, Jennifer Hasegawa beckons us into a world of surreal code where fairy tales braid with Buddhist spirituality, quantum science, and geomorphology, to weave a realm of delightful absurdity. Through adroit stanzas that echo like the voice of a white rabbit falling headlong beside us, Hasegawa leads us down, down, down, in an intimate tango with memory, familial history, and kinship, until we emerge changed.

—Ellen Chang-Richardson, author of *Blood Belies*

Hasegawa looks me dead in the eye and paints surreal scenes with a magical matter-of-factness that drags me through time and place like Hector behind the horse cart. Don't resist. You've worked hard enough today. Let her words wrap around your ankle and sweep you off to places you didn't know you didn't know—places too scary for nightmares and places so sweet that it hurts that they're imagined.

—Sunk Coast, musician and composer of the album *I felt the urge to push my hair to the side*

References of resentment, both residual and retired, ritualistic and religious, yet refereeing research that remains real. A reckoning of reality without resisting alien ghosts. Resolution or revolution? No, redemption. Jennifer Hasegawa continues the lineage of Kazuko Shiraishi but with the absence of linear time as in Shuri Kido.

—Shinji Eshima, the composer of the quintet, *Hymn for Her*

Library of Congress Cataloging-in-Publication Data
Names: Hasegawa, Jennifer, 1970- author.
Title: *Naomie Anomie : a Biography of Infinite Desire* / Jennifer Hasegawa.
Description: Oakland, California : Omnidawn Publishing, 2025. | Summary:
    "Jennifer Hasegawa's NAOMIE ANOMIE, A Biography of Infinite Desire, is an
    experimental poetic take on biography, growing increasingly surreal as
    it follows the truths behind its unreliable narrator through paradoxes
    rendered in luxurious detail. This book is a portrait of a flawed life,
    a call for attention to the looming omnicrisis, and a lyrical
    experiment in truth-telling. Feeling ever-increasing existential strain
    leading up to the COVID-19 pandemic and culminating in her decision to
    no longer venture outside of her apartment, Naomie is not surprised to
    find her name is an anagram for anomie, a term for the breakdown of
    social norms. In these pages is a meticulous account of everything that
    went wrong in Naomie's five decades of life. We find retellings of a
    life's most significant moments-not because they are sources of pride,
    but because they stand as the only decipherable moments of humanity amid
    a world of static. This story in verse acts as a survival guide, romance
    novel, liberation handbook, pulp thriller, and jokebook for those who
    will live through ongoing plagues, environmental change, total AI
    integration, water wars, and cyberattacks and who will come out the
    other side ready to restart"-- Provided by publisher.

Identifiers: LCCN 2024058447 | ISBN 9781632431653 (trade paperback)
Subjects: LCSH: Hasegawa, Jennifer, 1970- | LCGFT: Autobiographical poetry.
    | Poetry.
Classification: LCC PS3608.A78973 Z46 2025 | DDC 811/.6--dc23/eng/20241206
LC record available at https://lccn.loc.gov/2024058447

Published by Omnidawn Publishing, Oakland, California
www.omnidawn.com
10   9   8   7   6   5   4   3   2   1
ISBN: 978-1-63243-165-3

NAOMIE ANOMIE

A Biography of Infinite Desire

JENNIFER HASEGAWA

OMNIDAWN PUBLISHING

OAKLAND, CALIFORNIA

2025

For Dennis Jay

NAOMIE

AIM ONE

NAOMIE

from it to enter there is an expectation and you must break

Her First Word Was No

High-pitched moan
of domestication
in the rainforest
of nighttime.

Gallivanting bag
of innervated twigs
and strange balloons.

Closeted feral.

Feline teeth
in her brown rolls
of baby flesh
gave her night vision.

Each morning,
she watched father
open a tin of tuna
using a tiny opener,
like a folding quarter.

Returned it
to the same spot
on a shelf
on each day
of an entire life.

Things don't get lost
when they
stay put.

Body already half-dead,
No-No Cat disappeared
through the chili pepper hedge.

The faintest hiss and pop
of his beloved
decaying
rode on the wind for 49 days.

Father claims
to be going deaf,
but look at his face.

Hilo Shopping Center Easter Egg Hunt of 1976

Her first egg hunt
was a lesson
in war
and domination.

She returned
with one stepped-on
candy egg bursting
from its plastic suit.

Red dirt stuck
to fluffy white innards
meant for mouths.

She handed it to mother
who took one step
closer to death.

Hollow plastic eggs
equal power.

Why savage
for frivolous things.

How to escape this room
labeled
Born Weak.

She collapsed
into the lap
of the beautiful
superorganism.

Ants took her
in their shackles,
tiny amber jewels
eating this
accidental autocrat
into ash.

The ruddy-faced
apostle
who fed them
freshly churned butter
every Sunday
came running.

Tropical pietà;
Caucasian angel
held her like an autoharp
and sang her
into an urn.

Reconfigured by fire.

Fairy tale agape.
Body now a tabernacle
and never more willing
to lose.

Tombstone Read *Mama* Cuz They Forgot Her Given Name

They entered the forest
to find
a long-lost grave.

Father led
with a machete,
guided by an aunt
with magnetic grains
between the eyes.

Rusted out
car body.

Pile
of green glass
bottles.

Tombstones
of missionaries. One
a child.

Scales
of magnitude.

Bodies
given time and space—
disappear.

But everywhere,
the child came through
the kiawe trees.

Ashes to lashes,
dust to lust.
They sang it to scare
the big-time, red-eyed
shadow-stealer away.

Bottlebrush
and mosquito punk,
they scrubbed through
epochs of moss.

Glow of molten rock
seeped between branches
to illuminate
a true name.

Such monomythical sounds
made sluggish blood
flow free again.

Who here
thinks they are smarter
than spirit?

Who here
is not related
to the volcano?

Protagonist Runt / Antagonist Turn

She lies
ear to the floor
listening for mother's door
to open.

She tracks
the hem of mother's dress
pouring down
the front steps.

She monitors
the back of mother's car
until it turns the corner.

If she doesn't,
who knows.

Schrödinger's mother.

Schoolchildren
are herded into rooms
to be broken
of their lack of fear.

Those who've already
received the violence
of knowing
don't pay attention.

One unzips
his corduroys
to show her his work.

One unscrews
the top of a jar
to take the communion of paste.

One scans
the playground, growls:
I'm not terrible. You are.

Jello-dust sniffer.
Charming flagpole fighter.
Modern sociopath.
Animal cracker.

She remembers him
bashful and blushing
on picture day.

Who has not received
their daily serving
of canned apricots
and iron nails?

Raise your hand.

They Said Earthquake. She Heard Cupcake.

She couldn't follow instructions
because she couldn't hear them.

Who knew
it would be the happiest time
of her life.

They said she was naughty.
Then lazy.
Then the hospital room she shared
with another little girl.

Mary was from Palau
and had a bandage
over one eye.

Mary'd hold a finger
up to her lips
as she snuck out
of their room at night.

Fruit dove
in a white nightgown
weaving through the eaves.

Today, she still sees
Mary's one little eye,
signal lamp winking
in the dimlight.

Mischievous rhythm
and code. Insistent
on sovereignty
and nonstop playtime.

The Fingerpoke of Doom

Late night
in a box
floating in space.

Dazed in the flash
of the picture case.

When she turns the dial,
the whole place shakes.

Wrestler
in yellow underwear
tosses dolls around,
but they are people.

When they fall,
they bounce like balls,
but they are people.

She gave it all to the wolf
because it said it would bring her
10 times more.

There was a time when her mother
wrote down each thing
she'd held in her hands.

She coddled a kitten
till it was old enough
to live outside.

Nubby bike tires
creeping.

Drawstring bag
swinging.

Through thin muslin,
milky breath pushing.

Wolf loves
a freshly plucked heart,
last naive squeak
bubbling between its teeth.

Constructs a mental carnival
where it can ride tears
like a roller coaster.

Wolf doesn't want the ones
who see through the theatrics
of spray tans and oil-soaked hair.

It wants the ones
who'll shake hands
with a puff of smoke.

This Shell Game They Play Is Love

Her mother
was made
of pale jade
and ever-exhausted.

          Pluck key
          from bottom of can.

          Insert metal tab
          into slot.

Doling out
so much
punishment,
one woman
could not be expected
to do it all.

          Start turning.

          Separate
          top from bottom.

When a child
is punished,
it does not spoil.

It stays fresh
forever.
Obedient
as a canned good.

> Red
> as a scraped knee.

> So salty
> it smells like the time
> she nearly drowned.

If a mother gives in
to a child's demands,
a worm
will surely pop
out of its spoilt core.

Signing
with its
glossy pink body:

> I win.

The Fisher-Price of Fortune

The building
happened to have an elevator,
and so she rode in one
for the first time.

The doors opened
and closed
all on their own
and this compelled her.

Was the hand
on her shoulder
still her mother's?

They sat in a room
where mother and a stranger
faced off.

She felt her situation
correlated
to the spinning wheel
on television.

A harder
or softer tug
and she could've landed
in a place
she understood.

He said,
Go play
and extended an arm
toward everything
she'd ever wanted.

Deprivation
is the mother
of perversion.

Mouthwatering
plastics.

One body in the airplane.

One body in the schoolhouse.

One body in the castle
of suspicion
that is being
a child.

The Wheel of Sweet Leilani

Flying down the hill
in warm rain.
Wheels shimmy
with a wild sensation.

Tangled in a maze
of handlebars and spokes.
Still, her eyes tracked
to New Mother
turning away.

In a ring of light,
Old Mother arrived.
Lay her on the back
of Mr. Oba's sweet peach pony,
and rode her to safety.

Pink tissues
to wipe her tears.

Cuts cleansed
in a way that made her
want for more wounds.

Old Mother
lit a cigarette
from a pouch

with a metal mouth
that went click.

Two nodules
bent to fight
to keep things closed. Open.
Close. Open.
Close. Cycles imply
that something is
coming back.

Hers began at 8.
What did she know
of the chaos
of blood?

                    The girl smeared herself with it
                    to play dead.

                    This research is quantitative.

                    Imagine
                    you are in another world.

                    And you can choose
                    your ideal mother.

                    Which of these mothers
                    would you choose?

                    Which of them
                    would you never choose?

All the mothers
call from the tops
of hills.

Come home,
I am your mother,
whether we like it
or not.

AIM ONE

there is a deception and you must break from it to perceive

Deep in the Toy Box of Myths

Her favorite game
was the outlet
that sent fat vibrations
through her sweaty hand.

When kids came over,
they'd just fight
over the baby doll.

Who'd get to stuff it
under their T-shirt.

Who'd receive comfort
during the excruciating
birth show.

Big sister came calling
during a delivery.

This is how
it actually works.

It happens
when he carries your books.

It happens
when he promises to protect you.

It happens
when he kisses you on the lips
and you kick up your heel so hard
your slipper flies off.

Big sister
worked at her boyfriend's
jewelry shop.

One time,
she visited sister
and peered
into the velvet-lined
showcase window:

Two cane spiders
tangled
their long brown legs
and tumbled between
fake gold watches
and jade pendants
carved into
little dicks
and lucky frogs.

Hawai'i Geothermal Area

Father took a gig
as a guard
outside the new
geothermal plant.

He combed
the white curls
steaming from
the forest floor.

He sat alone
overnights in his rusting
truck bed.

Suntan Yellow.
Solidago.
Goldenrod
deadheaded
along the lower
East Rift Zone.

Midnight referee
to hippies,
money-makers,
and the earth's
molten core.

The one time
she saw him enraged:

Someone parked wrong;
blocked them in
at the county fair.

He pushed their car
until brilliant beams
shot from his shoulders
and sweat
ran down his temples
like raw milk.

                Strongest man in the world.

He ended up
hot-wiring it.
Moved it a foot.

                Smartest man in the world.

A policeman came.
His belt full of guns and chrome
squeaked as he bent over
to talk into father's window.

                Quietest man in the world.

Be careful
of the silent types,
mother said.
One day,
they'll just snap
and kill you.

Despite the spell
of spinning lights
and tinny calliope,
she thought she'd prefer it
to living
under a regime
of fickle moderation.

After the Old Hilo Wastewater Treatment Plant

They drove past
the water treatment plant
that stunk up the sweet air
that longed to reach
the rocky beaches
of Keaukaha.

All hail,
their rusty Datsun!
Tiny salvation,
carrying them with speed
out of the lagoon
overflowing
with discarded
one-eyed daruma dolls.

Nearly weightless
above an island
where you could still play
five-card stud with the spirits.

Crash test dummies
in the particle accelerator
of new power
and old fear,
the kind poor folks
can't help but hand down.

Mother's head flapped
like a rag in the wind.

Father's knees bloomed
with torch ginger.

And she
floated around the backseat
in a soap bubble
as adrenaline
taught her new things.

Where is it easiest
to hide the truth?

Their welcome mat read:

It's okay.
We don't want any trouble.

But inside,
they were mopping up
their own blood
and crafting splints
from guava branches
and string.

Dad told her,
Don't be afraid, girly.
You just have to make them think
you are.

Hatshepsut's Conception Was Through a Divine Wind

Neighbors set fire
to their garbage
in a big iron drum
right outside
her bedroom window.

What skills
might she learn
by inhaling
the discards
of others?

Mother says
she smells
her mother.

A wild boar,
black coat and snout glistening,
sits beside the hot drum,
growling into the evening.

The candle in her belly
catches. Her body,
a lantern obese
with premonitions
of cups,
both full
and broken.

Their eyes meet
through the smoke
exhaled by flames fed by
banana flower,
pork fat,
and the menses
of five daughters.

Let us give thanks
for this atmosphere,
possibly and soon
more fertile
than those
sucking it in.

Unko Raised His Fist

Her and Unko
went fishing
down South Point side,
near da hahd fo see place
dat get da long ropes
tied to precolonial
dimensions.

Unko said
fo no be sked.
Da buggah tied tight
to dis plane of existence.

Unko pitched dere tent inland
an den dey wen walk out to da cliffs
wit dere fishing gear.

Dey cast dere lines out like missiles
into megatons of ocean
dat get da bes kine fish fo catch,
like ulua, weke,
menpachi at night time,
perch, halalu.

Deres a lotta unknowns
dat come with
profound belief and beauty.

She glanced back at camp
and their tent was doing the hula
at sunset. Not 'auana kine,
but kahiko!

                "Da wind," Unko said.

Den da cast iron pan
dey was going use
fo fry da fish
leapt into the salty air.
Then up went the folding chairs.
Da bag charcoal
wen bus open
an look like one flock mynah birds
circling over camp.

                "Aisus," Unko said,
                "Da night marchers
                finally
                come for me."

She heard the ropes groan,
tightening in the pull
of the full moon tide.

                "Dey stay coming.
                Lie down,
                put yo face down,"
                Unko said.

Lava rock
punched her in the hard places
and drew blood
from the softest.

"No look!" Unko yelled.

The clanking faded eventually
and with that
Unko raised his fist
at the dawning place.

From the dark chaos
of the beforetimes came

light   sound   substance

that woke even
the sleepiest blood.

In the wreckage,
Unko opened his mouth
to shout, but out
came a tiny honu.

He launched it straight
off his tongue
into the yawing surf.

Every atom shimmered,
shook by the news
of this hard-won
truce.

Never Formally Learned. When Pressured Could Perform.

What these teens bore
driving donuts
in abandoned
sugarcane fields.

The copper dirt they inhaled
made them audacious
tropical alpinists.

Grandfathers they never met
surfed their fiberglass spoilers,
sickles in hand.

All they had
were cigarettes and schnapps
to get them
where they were asked to go.

Hoods hot
with the anarchy of pubarche
magnified by the presence
of ball lightning,
cascades of capillary
molten glass,
and termite wings.

Aching with Americana,
they caught migration in one hand,
forced metamorphosis in the other.

You Can Never Go Home Again, Also Can't Leave

One of her selves
went home
for the first time.

As it walked down the street,
two-legged dollies gawked
and regarded it
as alien.

It watched a sleek wooden vessel
launch into the bay
and regarded it
as alien.

It passed through
the five-and-dime
and was seduced
by the hot dog roller.

It wandered
into Tiny Town.
Maze of circular racks.
Each miniature outfit covered
in the thinnest plastic veil
made its arm hairs rise.

It returned to its hotel
on a dormant volcano.

So high it was,
it walked on clouds
to get to the lobby.

"Where am I?"
it asked.

"Are you stupid?"
said the concierge.

It looked outside.

A mongoose ran by
with an egg
in its mouth.

An ʻōhelo bush
was on fire.

"I am stupid,"
it agreed
and booked
the next flight out.

As it boarded,
it asked
that they destroy
the brakes
so there would be no
obstacles to departure.

The attendant
brought a tray
of a thousand lines,
one for each
promised communion
that never materialized.

With each insufflation,
it became clearer
that it would never return
to this place,
wherever it was,
if only the plane
would ever take off.

Extended Release of Teen Dreams

Sleep reunited them
at the interplanetary
lunch counter
in volumes of black
chemical lace
and a swinging
buttercup suit.

Red & green
cellophane loops
rode toothpicks
through their
club sandwich of stardust
on dark rye.

His bow tie undid itself
and hovered above them,
as if a drone.

They ran down
the boulevard
the way she thought
they would,
before she came
to know her station
through the reactions
of others.

They ducked
into a boutique
for black holes,
leaned across
melting glass and chrome
to sniff the pink liquid
of blow pop amnesia.

The sales clerk
presented a tray
of calculators.
He tested a sparkling
machine, long fingers
blurring across keys
in the calculus
of androgyny.
We'll take it!

In a rooftop cafe
above an interior city,
they played a game
of using little sticks
to make divots
in heavy paper.

Their warmth
came through
their clothing.

Cocktail of sleep
leaving, her face

went rigid. *Let's dance,*
he said,
grabbing her hands.

The fear
of gray chiffon.

She woke
with the feathers
of a great blue heron
clutched
in each fist.

Self-Soothing Lanugo

Dry-roasted
Dixie Runner
dysphoria capsule
rolls across
her tongue.

This is number 7.
Only 8 more to go
today.

She was hypnotized
to find the root cause:

                    Mother cowers
                    in a shadowy kitchen,
                    wooden spoon
                    beating back
                    a 10-foot box
                    of cake.

As a baby
she is locked
into a high chair
and already bored
by bodily functions.

                    Whose body
                    is this
                    anyway?

She forces mutations
that stop systems
and start new ones.

                    Ultra-typed ragdoll.

Exposure therapy
is a chalkboard
with 3 pristine
maxi pads stuck to it.

                    Is she X yet?

John in the drugstore
smells thin virginity.
Brandishes his weapon.

                    No one can defend her
                    because she is invincible.

When she grows up,
she wants to be an autotroph.

Mother says
there are so many games
to learn and play.

Candyland. Chess.
Mastermind. Speed.
Operation. Sorry. Life.

AIM EON

there is a symmetry and you must break from it to survive

Softness in a Place That's Inherently Unsafe

She wanted to weigh
as much as a soft white bunny
in a yellow sundress.

Then one day,
she turned sideways
to check herself
and she disappeared.

She received a rabbit
as a gift. They put it
in her arms. It was trembling
so hard and fast,
the condition
felt contagious.

Her father built it
a wire cage
on sturdy wooden legs
and put it in the garden.

She poked her finger
through a hole
to touch its silky fur.

It spun around
and bit.

She found the body
in the cage.

Something pursued it
through the wire floor
in a futile night
that still strangles
the wild lianas
of her mind.

It died
of fright.

Long and lean, it lay
like a piece
of damp driftwood.

Its fur
was drenched
in a sweat
that smelled
like baby powder,
like lighter fluid,
like infinite desire.

Each Planet an Eye in a Cosmic Slime

or The Flower Who Learned Telekinesis

The hair dryer
turned itself on
at midnight.

Ghosts don't knock,
they just move in.

Drag their feet.

She thinks
she's hearing things.

Wash their hands in static
before eating her secrets
like buttered corn
on the cob.

Succubus
of sublimations.

Sleep obediently
under her bed.
Then one day speak
while she's half asleep.

Mommy love
Mommy wash
Mommy sorry

Intergenerational
chromatophobic
horticulture.

She took her little shovel
and swallowed it.

Let the marigolds grow
around the mailbox.

Insatiable orange-haired
daughters of chaos.

Formulas
for true randomness
scrawled across their faces.

Say again
why modesty is worth it?

Say again
why she should want it?

Cataractous blue eye
of a giant—
can't even hold it
in her lonesome hand.

Does This Sexual Cannibalism Make Her Look Fat

From the first touch
of an unwashed hand,
a garden grew.

Shady delta of strangers.

It learned the patterns
of phone numbers
to female dorms.

                  Feet, tail,
                  wings, beak,
                  body feathers.

Dialpad sonations.
Rapid macroreversals
of beg and discard.

                  The value of rhythm
                  in birdsong
                  and the courtship
                  of beetles.

Starved
for the delicious nada.

Basking
in the luminous conceit
of gonads.

She drives fertility
like a founding father.

Witnesses the joy
of gonozooids
making a salad
of her future.

Not yet, it said,
as if asking for more time
on a playground swing.

The last thing
on the mind
of an orgasm
is the miracle
of childbirth.

Its machinations,
an ice cube in the knee pit.

Her body,
a controlled substance.

Increased risk of.

Black box warning
printed on the whites
of her eyes.

Plastic Surgery as a Conformative Response to Strain

Over dinner,
the surgeon asked him:
Do you want me
to make her
whole again?

Suddenly conscious
of her skin
like breading
on the cutlets
steaming on the table.

         Septate.
         Imperforate.
         Microperforate.
         Cribriform.

Give her to you
the way God intended.

         Tearaway flesh
         that lets the light in.
         Kaleidoscope
         of nothing.

She worried
that she'd sip
a café con leche

brought by the maid
and wake up
in hospital socks,
immaculate again.

From her bedroom window,
she saw the surrounding wall,
topped with thousands
of broken wine bottles.

She came to believe
she was a chuck roast
somehow shocked to life.

In the courtyard,
she watched
women in tangas
douse each other
with a hose
and disappear
in the refracting mist.

Allowed nothing else,
eventually,
she ate her own brain.

                    Super hot homo sacer.

Still,
people accuse her
of appropriation.

Telescopes Use Mirrors to Gather and Focus Light

Bob drew circles and squares
on a big screen.

She collected his timecard
and typed things up in triplicate.

He invited her to lunch.
She was so nervous
she forgot her purse.

What're you drawing
on your computer?
she said.

A spectrometer,
he said.
Oh, a spectrometer!

Do you know what that is?
he asked.
No. Tell me, Bob.

She gazed
into his blue eyes.
Hilda told her
he has a girlfriend
who told her
he spends all his time
looking in the mirror.

We're building a mirror
for a space telescope
to look deep
into the universe,
he said.

Oh,
she said.
What're you doing
this weekend?

Bob frowned at her,
like the time she wore
a denim dress
to the NASA awards dinner.

I'm buying a new car
and going to church,
he said.

How can you build
a space telescope
and believe in God?
she asked.

Bob got up and left.

She shouted after him,
Are you building a big mirror
so God can spend all his time
looking at himself?

He Claims the Transformer Is a Surveillance Camera

Comeback
L.A. Woman

Oozing from the tailpipe
of a Crown Victoria.

Police interceptor.

Red-lipped invader.

                    Driving down your freeways.

Careless and high
on binding intentions
into physical form.

                    Motel, honey, hoarder, madness.

Vulva towering
above Sunset.

                    Tops in copless bars.

Amulet
of athleticism.

Won 20 bucks
with a scratch card.

Pizza slices
and coke
on the curb.

Wacko truth serum.

Pissed the bed
and it felt like drowning.

Lifeguard Peggy.
Silver whistle.
Glitchy form
at the bottom
of the pool.

        So alone.

Forgot which laundry
had her interview suit.

        So alone.

He drove her around
examining utility poles.

        The hills are full of wire.

Pig head
in the market.
Eyes open.
Teeth glistening.

Where the best meat
comes from.

Once you taste it,
you won't be able to stop.

She expected
an endless loop
of imperceptible
atomic transitions.

But instead,
came transmissions
of blessings.

Patron Saint
of Doing-the-Best-You-Can.

Palliative salve
to the loneliest night hunters,
compulsively checking
the City of Light
for a time so good
they'll never have another.

Groundwater / Groundswell

After A.S.C.

Loyal
covert laundress,
A. washed out stains
and pressed panties
for first families:
Ford, Carter.
Reagan, Bush.

A few years
of the Clintons' clothes
and A. wrote to Barbara:
I'm retiring.

Silver Fox said: Stay.
We're coming back.

A party in the East Room
anointed Junior
next in line.

They've picked
the next president,
A. told her.

                Shake veil, shake
                to be seen. It's 1997
                and snowing in Queens.

Three years later,
Junior rode in,
right hand raised
and left hand
on the Sunshine State.

A freighter
idled in the deepwater harbor;
full of .22 caliber
Paraguayan nightshade.

They traffic in sleepwalking
and water. Rights
to 300,000 acres
of the Gran Chaco,
everywhere
the color of toast.

She's touched that land
where children
sell ground cherries
by the roadside.

Faces streaked with juice
and the brand of dust
that vibrates above
Acuífero Guaraní.

Water underground
rippling like backfat
in blackout pools

the size of three
Californias.

Psychopomp, ferry her.

Drink the ballot
as the blood of George.

Accept results
as the body of Abraham.

Adam, Eve, and exit polls.
Burning bush and ballot box.

It's the greatest show on Earth.
Vote. It's the real thing.

Stoners in the Hands of an Angry God

Zombie palm tree,
overpass melancholy,
and SigAlert Kaddish,
rate this interstate
on a scale of
1 to 10.

They mainlined
their bodies
7-lanes wide.
She threw her purse
out the window.

Goodbye self!

She looked to him
and he had horns.
He looked to her
and she had four.

Demons arrive late.
Their maps contain
all dimensions.

They reached the beach
to climb sand dunes
while insomniac citizens
slept, dreaming

of body snatchers
and moving money.

Toeing the droning shore,
she lifted her shirt
for a ghostly light
beaming from her navel.

The Pacific lay
non-Newtonian
beneath their feet
and so they walked
a straight line
to Point Dume.

Nuclear reactions
held hands
to broadcast stories
of great bears
and damned maidens
chained to sea rocks.

By sunrise,
her pupils small
and horns fallen away,
a stream of tiny paper tabs
flew out of her mouth.

On each, a dragon
sent to bite through
her dull chains.

But instead,
they held her tighter,
together spitting teeth
and rubbing their gums
along the rocky shore.

If Successful They Fall to the Ground and Die

The matriarch
threw the gravy boat
against the kitchen wall
and told everyone
to go to hell.

Then, she got on the porch swing
and swung so high
they never saw her again.

From the outside, [   ]
looked so inviting.
On the inside,
nothing could survive.

The girl closed her eyes
and translucent brown drippings
lullabied her to sleep.

The moon hid
its full white body.

Tides cried
over the weight
of so much water.

Morbidly obese infidels
of the church
of smallness.

Poppies unbloomed,
trapping workers
into stinging stamens
until their honeyed guts
sent signals.

At sunrise,
blossoms reopened,
spilling bodies
like whole cloves.

Antidote
to disciplined nightbirds
flying themselves
into the ground.

Just a spoonful
and she moved faster
than the speed of light.

Mass impossibly infinite.

There is carnage
in the battle
to love a body.

She broke the laws
of physics
with her own bones
to escape the gravity
of all she didn't need.

ANOMIE

there is a compulsion and you must break from it to escape to there

Dear Acid Wash,

A sesamoid is a bone
stuffed into a tendon.

> You don't know
> what things are called
> until you break them.

Open sesame!

The satanic meeting
she went to
thinking it was
a book club.

Velvet robes, 666,
and the biscuit
she spit out
after a guy told her
it had his blood in it.

> You act like
> you don't know
> you've won the lottery.

They loaded her
into an armored truck
they mistook
for an ambulance.

Everyone wore
built-in handcuffs
at this hospital.

They put a skateboard
in the bed next to hers.
Cracked clean in half,
it called out,
"I want my mama!"

A nurse checked its trucks
and said,
"She's in a drained-out pool
in Costa Mesa."

They swaddled the pieces
in grip tape
and lay the crying detritus
in her dread-laden arms.

These days
they make prosthetics
for anything you've lost.

She used to wish
she was someone else.
Now, she doesn't have to.

The Big Wheel Rolling Over Her
On Metempsychosis

Her rib cage
is a volcano
treated as a dumbwaiter.

                              Deliver coffee
                              to room 3.

                         Take steaks
                         to suite 8.

                    Dump undershirts
                    in the basement.

               Wipe yourself clean
               and hang still
               till the morning rush.

Hidden nautilus.
Chamber of cheeseburger
myths. Forge of air hose
and raw cream.

This antidream
of vaginalia
trained on petroleum
and gardenias
dropping
from a pipette.

Is she a meal
floating in midair
or a perfect machine?

Yesterday,
she needed some money.

Today,
she is a dollar bill.

Cold Turkey Mother

Mother doesn't remember
the fentanyl patches
Father pasted so carefully
to her back.

Father wore gloves
and tracked the dates and times
of application.
Daughter remembers
his stark handwriting
on the packets.

Father taught Daughter
about signatures:
You need one
to prove it's you.
Don't make it nice.
Make it messy.

Mother fell
in the kitchen
chasing the poodle.
Vertebrae collapsed.

They gave her
oxycodone
and when the dose
could go no higher,
fentanyl.

When Daughter visited,
Mother slept most of the time.
When Mother was awake,
Mother was still asleep.

Mother said she stopped
wearing the patches
because they dulled
her taste buds.
She wanted to taste again.

Mother said
her back's so bent
she can't
look out the window.

Mother doesn't remember
the fentanyl patches
Father pasted so carefully
to her back.

Quantum Radical Pair Mechanism

Feeling
so wicked
for what
they'd done,
her hands
flew clean away.

A pair
of topaz doves
startled
by the calling
of their
own names. And how
were they named?

                            Everything
                            and always.

So far afield,
she split in two,
throwing off
even a divine
dead reckoning.

Raise
a bamboo pole
flying a red rag,
tall enough
to tickle
the Kármán line.

Every set of lips
she'd kissed
tore like breadcrumbs
and winged a path
to her front trapdoor.

Huddled in the dark,
they gnawed on her shame;
shedding the bitter spines
of truthgrass
and unclaimed names.

He Asked Her to Fax Sir Arthur C. Clarke
After S.B.

Every Sunday,
a voice draws open draperies
up and down her block.

From the interstellar street corner:
the sounds of devotion.

Aleluya
to the father of fishes,
the father of fishers,
the father of fishmongers!

His father was a pilot;
a bus driver in the sky.
And so he studied the sky.

There are three fishes
hidden in the city
and they must find them.

The first is made of glass
and represents health.

The second is made of stone
and represents knowledge.

The third is made of flesh
and represents a god

to be created,
but not worshipped.

They found the fishes
and he ate all three.

When you've provided proof
of the invisible,
they'll let you do anything.

Aleluya
to the father of dark matter,
to the son of tenuous gases,
to the holy ghost
of the hot corona.

When the Future Looks Like a Forest

She said
to her lover:
Are you really a tree
or do you just play one
on TV?

When Wattieza
painted its likeness,
the thing became human,
and so ancestral tree matter
flows through
her sympathetic system.

Methuselah pine,
Cypress of Abarqu, and
Llangernyw Yew:
Non-clonal agents
from whom she learned
to fight or fly.

Trees churn
deep soil,
proceed along
underground rivers;
slow-grazing
cellulose buffalo.

They have
sharp voices;
sound like
thick paper bags
flicked open.

Their rings: their mouths.

Trees telescope
through millennia.

Show up
like old light.

Branches
tickling scars
even she forgot
she hid,
deep inside
the hard bark
of her body.

O Placenta

Hovering
over dark hills,
flying saucer
so thick in the middle
with blood.

Vigilant
over soft crops.
Eight billion bipeds.
All failures of the flesh
before
this singular perfection
lay hidden in the rocks.

Bat, pangolin, whale,
elk, opossum, human.

Warm-blooded,
fur-bearing,
live young-suckling;
bound for ghost lineage
neverland.

She's so self-centered.

When whales breastfeed,
their milk
thick as toothpaste
floats in water.

She's so self-centered.

When marsupials mate,
a bifurcated penis
enters two vaginas
connected to two uteruses.
Glory
a baby emerges
from a third
and transient
canal.

She's so self-centered.

When she was inside
she herself
was a foreign body.
If she touched
her home of tissue and bone,
its cells
would have devoured her.
Little bean,
capable of what?

O placenta!
Love song
to an ancient retrovirus
that laid down
the good grounds
for immune privilege.

Hidden virality.
Domesticated,
mutating,
and free to roam.

Dawn mother arrived
in her purple river car.
Hips wide enough
to bear the earth.

Afterbirth eaten
under neon signs
flashing food, gas,
and clean restrooms.

Add to three cups milk
and drink. Drink the elixir
of connected
destinies.

What you say
is a hallucination
and real machines
can't look you in the eye.

When viruses communicate,
they don't have to lie.

In Her Dreams, She Radiates

Defiant
as the dreamlife
of strontium;
the half-life
of brains.

What might
a confidence man
manifest,
tied to a chariot
drawn by donkeys.

Amniotic afterlives
flow through
Pape'ete,
Plymouth,
Pryp'yat',
primordial whatnot.

Satellite photographs
reveal a parade
of ghosts
on the river.

They tell her
about the way
atoms travel.

One might say
she is a body
of the Holocene.

Plasticine shape-shifter
built from ancestors
one slow cell
at a time.

One might say
the Zone of Alienation
is relatively safe to visit.

When we hug there,
we disappear.

Notes

NAOMIE ANOMIE: *Anomie* refers to a state of normlessness where societal norms are unclear or absent, often arising during rapid social or economic changes. This lack of clear norms can cause psychological distress and alienation, as well as increased deviance, as individuals struggle to achieve societal goals without adequate or well-defined guidelines.

Her First Word Was No: This poem includes the line *rode on the wind for 49 days.* In Buddhist tradition, forty-nine days mark a critical period after death, believed to be the time it takes for the soul of the deceased to transition from this world to the next or be reborn. This period involves several rituals and prayers to help guide and support the deceased's soul through its journey, culminating in a final ritual on the 49th day to ensure a peaceful rebirth or entry into nirvana.

Protagonist Runt / Antagonist Turn: This poem includes the lines *Who has not received | their daily recommended serving | of canned apricots | and iron nails?* In *Farewell to Manzanar*, Jeanne Wakatsuki Houston described her first meal at the Manzanar War Relocation Center, one of ten American concentration camps where more than 120,000 Japanese Americans were incarcerated during World War II. She described it as, "canned Vienna sausage, canned string beans, steamed rice that had been cooked too long, and on top of the rice a serving of canned apricots."

Captain James Cook's voyages to Hawaiʻi marked the first sustained European contact with the Hawaiian Islands. His arrival coincided with the Makahiki festival, a time dedicated to Lono, the Hawaiian god of fertility, agriculture, and peace. This led the Hawaiians to misidentify Cook as the god Lono and treat him with great reverence and hospitality. Fascinated by iron, the Hawaiians engaged in trade with Cook's crew, exchanging cultural and personal items, including sexual favors, for pieces of iron and iron nails. Ultimately, Cook was killed in Kealakekua Bay, Hawai'i in 1779. Cook attempted to take a Hawaiian chief hostage to recover a stolen ship's boat. To defend the chief, the Hawaiians struck Cook on the head with a leiomano shark-toothed club and stabbed him with a metal dagger they obtained through trade with Cook's crew.

They Said Earthquake. She Heard Cupcake: This poem includes the line *Mary was from Palau*. In the 1970s, Palau was on the journey toward independence from the Trust Territory of the Pacific Islands under US administration. This transition was characterized by significant shifts, including increased interactions with the US, notably in sectors such as healthcare, where Palauans often received medical services in American facilities, including those in Hawai'i. Such arrangements were reflective of the broader US influence across the Pacific, which instilled both opportunities and a pervasive sense of uncertainty about the future. Palau's reliance on American aid may have limited economic self-sufficiency. Cultural and environmental impacts due to prolonged American presence may have also posed challenges, potentially altering traditional lifestyles and environmental integrity.

The Wheel of Sweet Leilani: The passage beginning with *This research is quantitative* includes found language from "How Children See their Parents—A Short Intergeneration Comparative Analysis" by Ioana Lepadatu, Spiru Haret University, Bucharest. This research explores how perceptions of parents have changed over different generations and analyzes how cultural, social, and economic shifts influence children's views of their parents' roles and behaviors.

Hawai'i Geothermal Area: This poem is partially set at a geothermal plant on the lower East Rift Zone of Kīlauea volcano. It refers to geothermal energy production on the Big Island of Hawai'i that began in the 1970s, driven by abundant volcanic activity, particularly around Kīlauea volcano known for its continuous lava flows. The first successful geothermal well was drilled in 1976 in the Puna district, leading to the establishment of the Puna Geothermal Venture in the 1980s. This venture met with mixed reactions from the local community. While some residents and officials viewed the development as a valuable source of clean energy and local jobs, others were concerned about environmental impacts and the desecration of sacred land. These concerns led to protests and opposition, prompting the need for heightened security measures to ensure the safety of the site and its workers.

After the Old Hilo Wastewater Treatment Plant: This poem includes the lines *overflowing | with discarded | one-eyed | daruma dolls*. Daruma dolls are traditional Japanese talismans symbolizing perseverance and good luck, inspired by Bodhidharma, the founder of Zen Buddhism. These hollow, round, red dolls are often bought without pupils painted in the eyes. Owners paint one pupil when they set a goal and the other when the goal is achieved, reflecting the theme of persistence and fulfillment.

Hatshepsut's Conception Was Through a Divine Wind: Hatshepsut, one of ancient Egypt's few female pharaohs, was said to be conceived through a divine wind in the form of an ankh, a symbol of life, carried by the god Amun who appeared as her father. This miraculous birth narrative served to legitimize her rule in a patriarchal society, reinforcing her divine right to the throne. Hatshepsut distinguished herself by successfully ruling Egypt in peace and prosperity and expanding trade networks. She also initiated the restoration of many temples and religious structures that had fallen into disrepair, solidifying her image as a pharaoh deeply committed to her people's spiritual welfare.

Unko Raised His Fist: This poem includes the lines *Her and unko | went fishing | down South Point side*. South Point, known locally as Ka Lae, on the

Big Island of Hawai'i, is the southernmost point in the United States. This rugged and windswept region features steep cliffs that drop sharply into the Pacific Ocean, making it a popular spot for reel fishing directly from the shore. Fishers at South Point often use the unique method of securing themselves with harnesses to the cliffs to cast their lines into the deep, fish-rich waters below, exploiting the location's unique geographical and oceanic currents.

This poem includes the lines *and their tent was doing the hula | at sunset. Not 'auana kine, | but kahiko!* Kahiko hula is the ancient style characterized by traditional chants, percussion instruments, and natural attire, featuring strong, grounded movements and rhythmic footwork. In contrast, 'auana hula, meaning "to wander," is a modern adaptation with melodic music and string instruments like the ukulele, showcasing smooth, flowing movements that travel across the floor. One might sense a contrast between the percussive energy of kahiko and the melodic fluidity of 'auana.

Never Formally Learned. When Pressured Could Perform.: This poem includes the lines *magnified by the presence | of ball lightning.* Ball lightning is a rare and mysterious phenomenon where a spherical, glowing orb of electricity appears during thunderstorms, seeming to float or move erratically through the air. On the Big Island of Hawai'i, some legends attribute ball lightning to supernatural causes rather than weather or scientific explanations, often viewing these luminous spheres as manifestations of the gods or spirits.

The poem also includes the lines *cascades of capillary | molten glass | and termite wings.* Capillary molten glass, also known as Pele's hair, is a unique volcanic glass, resembling thin, delicate strands of hair. It forms when molten lava is ejected into the air and rapidly stretched by the wind into long fibers that solidify upon cooling. Pele is revered in Hawaiian mythology as the goddess of volcanoes and fire, the creator of the Hawaiian Islands, and a powerful deity embodying both creation and destruction.

You Can Never Go Home Again, Also Can't Leave: This poem includes the lines *It returned to its hotel / on a dormant volcano*. This hotel is meant to be Pohakuloa Training Area, a military training camp located on the Big Island of Hawai'i, situated between Mauna Loa, Mauna Kea, and the Hualalai volcanic mountains. The camp is at an elevation of approximately 6,800 feet above sea level, making it one of the highest military camps in the US. Due to its high elevation, Pohakuloa often sits above the cloud cover, which can result in clear skies overhead while clouds accumulate at lower altitudes around the surrounding mountain slopes.

Extended Release of Teen Dreams: This poem includes the lines *The fear / of gray chiffon*. These are misheard lyrics from "Let's Dance" by David Bowie: *For fear your grace should fall*.

Self-Soothing Lanugo: Lanugo is a type of fine, soft hair that typically covers the body of a fetus and usually sheds before birth. In adults, it can regrow due to anorexia or other conditions that lead to severe malnutrition. The body produces lanugo in an attempt to conserve heat and regulate body temperature due to the loss of insulating body fat.

The poem includes the line *Ultra-typed ragdoll*. It refers to a Ragdoll cat that is the result of selective or extreme breeding to produce even more specific or striking features that its breed is known for, including a docile, floppy nature.

Plastic Surgery as a Conformative Response to Strain: This poem's title includes the word *Strain*. It refers to Merton's Strain Theory, which suggests that societal structures can pressure individuals when there is a gap between culturally defined goals and the means available to achieve them, leading to various adaptive responses: conformity, innovation, ritualism, retreatism, and rebellion.

This poem includes these lines: *Septate. / Imperforate. / Microperforate. / Cribriform*. These are hymen types; a hymen being the thin membrane located at the vaginal opening, and its appearance can vary widely. The septate hymen has an extra band of tissue creating two openings. The imperforate hymen completely covers the vaginal opening, blocking it. The microperforate hymen has a very small opening. The cribriform hymen has multiple small openings.

This poem includes the line *Super hot homo sacer*. *Homo sacer* translates to "sacred man" in Latin. The term refers to a person in ancient Roman law who is considered sacred in the sense that they are set apart and cannot be sacrificed in religious rituals, but can be killed without legal repercussions. This creates a paradoxical status where the individual is both sanctified and excluded from legal and social protections.

He Claims the Transformer Is a Surveillance Camera: This poem includes the lines *Patron Saint / of Doing-the-Best-You-Can*. This is Santa Monica who lends her name to the city of Santa Monica and its major artery, the Santa Monica Freeway, in Los Angeles.

Groundwater / Groundswell: This poem includes the lines *that vibrates above / Acuífero Guaraní*. The Bush family reportedly purchased 121,407 hectares of land in Paraguay, which is situated over a section of the Acuífero Guaraní/Guarani Aquifer, one of the world's largest freshwater reserves. This strategic acquisition places the family atop a critical resource in the Gran Chaco region, highlighting concerns about the influence of private ownership over essential water supplies. The land and aquifer under it span across Paraguay, Argentina, Brazil, and Uruguay, making it a significant point of interest in discussions about water security and sovereignty in the region.

Stoners in the Hands of an Angry God: This poem includes the lines *The Pacific lay / non-Newtonian / beneath their feet*. Non-Newtonian fluids are substances that change their viscosity or flow behavior under stress. Unlike water or oil, which have consistent flow characteristics, non-Newtonian fluids can become either more liquid or more solid when shaken, stirred, or otherwise stressed.

The Big Wheel Rolling Over Her: On Metempsychosis: *Metempsychosis* is a belief that the soul can transfer from one body to another after death, not only inhabiting human or animal forms but potentially inanimate objects as well. This concept, found in various spiritual and philosophical traditions, suggests that the soul's journey through different bodies, including objects like stones or plants serves as a means for spiritual learning and evolution. Through these diverse experiences, the soul may grow and evolve across numerous lifetimes.

Quantum Radical Pair Mechanism: The quantum radical pair mechanism is a theory in physics and chemistry that describes how pairs of molecules with unpaired electrons (radical pairs) can interact in ways that depend on their quantum states, which are sensitive to magnetic fields. This mechanism is believed to help certain animals, like birds, navigate by detecting Earth's magnetic field, guiding them during migration.

This poem includes the lines *tall enough / to tickle / the Kármán line.* The Kármán line is an imaginary boundary about 100 kilometers (62 miles) above the Earth's surface that marks the edge of space. This line is used to distinguish between Earth's atmosphere and outer space for regulatory and record-keeping purposes, such as determining when astronauts earn their wings.

He Asked Her to Fax Sir Arthur C. Clark.: S.B. is Dr. Stuart Bowyer. He was best known for his trailblazing work in the field of extreme ultraviolet (EUV) astronomy. This range of the electromagnetic spectrum is crucial for studying the hot and energetic processes in the universe, such as those occurring in the atmospheres of stars or around black holes. Dr. Bowyer's work significantly advanced our understanding of these cosmic phenomena and contributed to numerous discoveries in the field of astrophysics.

Dr. Bowyer died from complications of COVID-19 on September 23, 2020. He was 86.

When the Future Looks Like a Forest: This poem includes references to each of the following extraordinary trees.

Wattieza: This is the world's oldest known tree and the earliest known large, tree-forming plant. Discovered as fossils, Wattieza trees lived over 385 million years ago and are significant for providing insights into the early development of forest ecosystems on Earth.

Methuselah pine: This ancient bristlecone pine tree is located in California's White Mountains and is often cited as one of the oldest living non-clonal organisms in the world, with an age of over 4,800 years. Non-clonal means that the organism, such as a tree, has grown and survived as an individual from a single seed rather than reproducing through cloning.

Cypress of Abarqu: Located in Iran, it is believed to be over 4,000 years old. It is significant not only for its age but also as a cultural and historical symbol in Iran.

Llangernyw Yew: Located in Wales, it is estimated to be between 4,000 to 5,000 years old, making it one of the oldest living organisms in the United Kingdom.

O Placenta: The mammalian placenta originated from a genetic mutation introduced by an ancient retrovirus. This mutation helped form the placenta by enabling cells to fuse together, creating a special layer that allows vital nutrients and oxygen to pass from mother to fetus. This development significantly advanced mammalian reproduction by allowing embryos to grow within the mother's body, leading to safer, more controlled gestation periods. The presence of the placenta supports more complex fetal development and has been key to the evolutionary success of mammals.

Acknowledgments

Thank you, Rusty Morrison, for your deep reading and intuitive guidance, which enabled this work to realize its full intention.

Thank you, Shanna Compton, for your artistry and expertise, which brought the interior of this book to its authentic life.

Thank you, Laura Joakimson and everyone at Omnidawn, for your generous care and dedication, which manifested this work.

Thank you, Ken Keegan, for co-founding Omnidawn with Rusty Morrison in 2001. Your impact on poetry endures.

About the Author

Jennifer Hasegawa is a poet and information architect whose first book of poetry, *La Chica's Field Guide to Banzai Living,* won the Joseph Henry Jackson Literary Award from the San Francisco Foundation and was long-listed for *The Believer* Book Award.

She edited *Mr. Omoshiroi: Notes from a Sansei Babyboomer and Bonsai Sensei,* the autobiography of Dennis Makishima.

Jennifer is also the founder of *Kau Kau Chronicles* (www.kaukauchronicles.org), a project dedicated to preserving and sharing recipes from out-of-print cookbooks published by Hawai'i community organizations from the early 1900s to the early 2000s.

Her work has appeared in *The Adroit Journal, Bamboo Ridge, Bennington Review, jubilat, Tule Review, takahē,* and *Vallum.*

A third-generation Japanese American born and raised on the Big Island of Hawai'i, Jennifer now lives in San Francisco.

NAOMIE ANOMIE: *A Biography of Infinite Desire*
by Jennifer Hasegawa
Cover design by Jennifer Hasegawa
Interior design by Shanna Compton

Cover typefaces:
Interior typefaces: Freight Sans Pro and Freight Text Pro

Printed in the United States
by Books International, Dulles, Virginia
on Acid-Free Archival Quality Recycled Paper

Publication of this book was made possible in part by gifts from
Katherine & John Gravendyk in honor of Hillary Gravendyk,
Francesca Bell, Mary Mackey, and The New Place Fund

Omnidawn Publishing   Oakland, California
Staff and Volunteers, Spring 2025
Rusty Morrison & Laura Joakimson, co-publishers
Rob Hendricks, poetry & fiction editor, post-pub marketing
Jeffrey Kingman, copy editor
Sharon Zetter, poetry editor & book designer
Anthony Cody, poetry editor
Liza Flum, poetry editor
Rayna Carey, poetry editor
Sophia Carr, production editor
Elizabeth Aeschliman, fiction & poetry editor
Jennifer Metsker, marketing assistant
Avantika Chitturi, marketing assistant
Angela Liu, marketing assistant